Best Easy Day Hikes
South Bay L.A.

Allen Riedel

FALCON GUIDES

GUILFORD, CONNECTICUT
HELENA, MONTANA

AN IMPRINT OF GLOBE PEQUOT PRESS

FALCONGUIDES®

TOPO! Explorer software and SuperQuad source maps courtesy of
National Geographic Maps. For information about TOPO! Explorer,
TOPO!, and Nat Geo Maps products, go to www.topo.com or www
.natgeomaps.com.

Project editor: Julie Marsh
Layout artist: Kevin Mak
Maps: Off Route Inc. © Morris Book Publishing, LLC

Library of Congress Cataloging-in-Publication Data
Riedel, Allen.
  Best easy day hikes, South Bay L.A. / Allen Riedel.
    p. cm. – (FalconGuides)
  ISBN 978-0-7627-5259-1
  1. Hiking–California–Los Angeles–Guidebooks. 2. Trails–California–
Los Angeles–Guidebooks. 3. Los Angeles (Calif.)–Guidebooks. I.
Title.
  GV199.42.C22L6568 2009
  917.94'940454–dc22

                                              2009030643

Printed in the United States of America
10 9 8 7 6 5 4 3 2 1

For Sierra, Makaila, and Michael

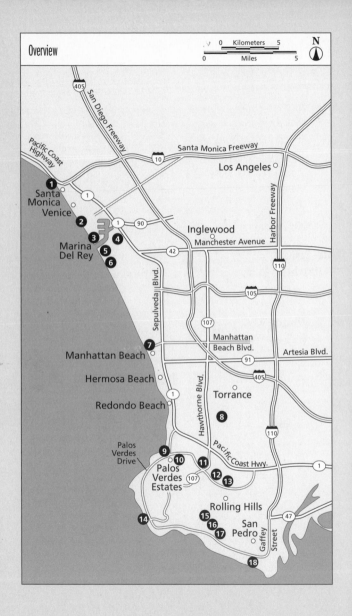

Contents

Help Us Keep This Guide Up to Date

Every effort has been made by the author and editors to make this guide as accurate and useful as possible. However, many things can change after a guide is published—trails are rerouted, regulations change, facilities come under new management, etc.

We would love to hear from you concerning your experiences with this guide and how you feel it could be improved and kept up to date. While we may not be able to respond to all comments and suggestions, we'll take them to heart and we'll also make certain to share them with the author. Please send your comments and suggestions to the following address:

> Globe Pequot Press
> Reader Response/Editorial Department
> P.O. Box 480
> Guilford, CT 06437

Or you may e-mail us at:

> editorial@GlobePequot.com

Thanks for your input, and happy trails!

Acknowledgments

I would like to first and foremost thank all of the people who have spent time hiking with me through mountains, deserts, hills, forests, jungles, and coastal beaches. Many of you, my friends, have inspired me in countless ways, and I can't thank you enough. I would like to mention some of you by name: Monique Riedel, Sean Coolican, Adam Mendelsohn, Cameron Alston, Bill Buck, Matt Piazza, Bruno Lucidarme, Chrissy Ziburski, Eric Walther, Bob Romano, Michael Millenheft III, Sierra Riedel, Makaila Riedel, Jim Zuber, Danny Suarez, Dylan Riedel, Eric Romero, Donn DeBaun, Alex Wilson, Dawn Wilson, and Jane Weal.

I would also like to acknowledge my family: Monique, Michael, Sierra, and Makaila. All four of you have spent lots of time with me on trails that were great and some "not so much". . . . I love you with all my heart.

I also owe a lot to my mom and dad, Barbara and Elmer Riedel, who raised me to believe in myself. Thanks!

Thanks to my brother, Larry; my grandparents, Herbert and Vivian Ward and Elmer and Lucille Riedel; and my in-laws, Anna and Richard Chavez. I am a better person because of all of you.

I am also grateful for the opportunities that I have been granted by writing for the most amazing Web site: www.localhikes.com. It seems Jim Zuber has been my biggest resource in the writing world, and I can never thank him enough for the awesome site and the amount of work he has sent my way. You rule, Jim!

I would like to thank Dave Ammenheuser and Patricia Mays at the Press Enterprise, who have been great editors and incredible to work for.

I would like to thank Scott Adams and the wonderful people at Globe Pequot Press, as well as my other publisher, The Mountaineers Books. Ashley, Kate, Carol, and everyone there have always been spectacular.

I would also like to thank Scott Ammons and all the terrific people at REI. It has been great getting started as an Outdoor School instructor.

Lastly, I would like to thank all of the students and teachers I have worked with over the past ten years. It has been a joy knowing all of you.

Introduction

This book contains eighteen easy day hikes situated in and around the South Bay of Los Angeles County—what locals often refer to as Southland. The hikes are located in a variety of areas ranging from state, county, and city parks to private land. The book highlights the best short and easy hikes in the region.

The South Bay is a decidedly urbane region that stretches from the southern portion of Santa Monica Bay to San Pedro Bay and Long Beach. Bounded by West LA to the north and the Gateway Cities to the east, the area is mainly made up of beach cities, and coastline predominates most of the hiking in the vicinity.

Not many stretches of wild and open land exist in the area, though there are ample opportunities for getting outdoors and hiking. One has to be a little creative in some of the endeavors, but quite a few short and brisk trips can be strung together with minimal detours through dense civilization. The coast is extravagant; mansions and affluence adorn much of the landscape.

Named for its location relative to the rest of Los Angeles County, the South Bay is a conglomeration of cities, towns, and other incorporated areas. Primarily suburban, some of the cities in the region have a comfier, slower paced feel than the usual Los Angeles County fare, but the region itself is much more heavily populated than other parts of the United States, and outsiders will probably not notice much difference between the cities within the urban region and those in the suburbs. Travel to more northern and perhaps more hiker-friendly climes is exaggerated due to Los

Angeles traffic, making it all the more important to seek out places to hike within the immediate vicinity.

Typically Southern Californian, the South Bay sits on the ocean edge of a semiarid Mediterranean ecosystem, ringed by the mountains uplifted from the tectonic forces of the San Andreas Fault. Weather patterns shift frequently, and the area can be socked in with fog any time of year. Rains typically fall from November through February, though generally not for long periods of time or in large amounts.

Hiking and exercising in the region is a popular activity, especially in the early morning and evening during summertime, and throughout the day during the fall, winter, and spring. Depending upon the cloud cover and temperature, summer days can be pleasant or absolutely desiccating.

While wildlife is sparse in the area, you may see some, but nothing presents much of a danger except for the possibility of rattlesnakes and spiders. Do not walk through tall grass or place hands and feet into locations unseen. Snakes are afraid of humans, and they understand the world through sensing vibrations. Typically, snakes will be alerted and flee long before a human approaches on the trail. Rattlesnakes will only strike if threatened, so the best thing to do is back away or walk in a wide berth around them on the trail. Small mammals such as squirrels, skunks, possums, and mice also inhabit the region.

Insects are not normally a problem in the South Bay, though after rains ticks can present a small problem, as can mosquitoes and other pests. Flies and gnats can be slightly troublesome in wetter areas, but are not normally a nuisance. A mild insect repellent should do the trick for most hikes, and dogs should be protected with proper vaccinations and pet medicines. Watch out for poison oak, with its three-pronged leaves. Its toxic oil, urushiol, is difficult to remove and can be spread if skin and clothing are not thoroughly cleansed after contact. Take care to avoid the plant.

Weather

The South Bay is mostly semiarid, though coastal areas and the lower elevations can be hot but pleasant during the months of June, July, August, and September. Fog, wind, and cold can be a factor any time of year, so hikers should be prepared for quick changes in weather. Heat can also be an issue year-round, though late October through May are generally milder even in the hotter parts of the region.

Rain is not the normal state of affairs in Southern California, and the South Bay is no exception, getting between 10 and 12 inches annually. The rainy season is typically from November through February, with showers more likely during December and January. Most rainstorms are over as quickly as they begin, though the region does see periods of continuing rainfall during the winter.

Summer temperatures can reach triple digits, though the coastal cities rarely rise above the 80s. The best times of year to hike in the South Bay are fall through spring, when the temperatures are mild during the day. Early morning just before and after sunrise and evening right before and after sunset are pleasant in the summer almost anywhere.

Preparing for Your Hike

Before you go hiking, always be prepared. Let someone know where you are planning to go, and leave an itinerary of your hiking destination with a reliable friend. Provide an expected return time and the name of the trailhead you are visiting, along with the specific route you will be taking. Be sure that your friend will contact authorities should you not return when expected.

Water is essential. Hydrate before you leave and during your hike, and leave extra water in your vehicle so you can hydrate upon return. A good rule of thumb for hiking is one-half to one liter per hour of hiking, and on hot days without shade, you should drink as much as one gallon per hour of hiking. Salty snacks can help with water retention. Avoid overexertion during the hottest part of the day.

When you hike, you should bring along the "Ten Essentials" to provide yourself with the basic necessities for survival should the unexpected occur:

1. Navigation (map, compass, GPS)
2. Sun protection (hat, sunscreen)
3. Insulation (layered clothing)
4. Illumination (head lamp, flashlight)
5. First-aid supplies (Band-Aids, bandages, gauze, tape, tweezers, etc.)
6. Repair kit and tools (knife, duct tape, etc.)
7. Nutrition (extra food)
8. Hydration (extra water)
9. Emergency shelter (tarp, tent, sleeping bag, or emergency blanket)
10. Fire starter (necessary for life-threatening emergencies only)

Hiking is a relatively safe activity, especially when care is taken, although it is always best to prepare for any eventuality. Minor mishaps like taking a wrong turn, getting back after dark, or being lost for a short while can be frightening, but as long as cool heads prevail, most outdoor situations can be easily rectified. The Ten Essentials are designed to keep people safe and provide a backup plan should something go wrong.

The South Bay is heavily populated, and the hikes in this book are centered in areas where others congregate. There aren't really any true "wilderness" hikes to be found in the South Bay, and most of these trails will be frequently traveled by others, limiting the necessity of many of the Ten Essentials. It should be noted, however, that anything can happen, so the more prepared you are, the better off you will be should a situation occur.

Other items may be fun to have along as well. Cameras can be used to record an excursion for posterity, while binoculars come in handy for wildlife viewing. Plant, bird, mammal, and insect identification guides can prove to be informative and educational. Handheld global positioning satellite units are becoming more and more inexpensive and are a great tool to use on the trail. Maps should be taken, but most trails are well marked.

Clothing, Shoes, and Gear

Clothing should be made up of layers to protect your body from the elements, whether wind, heat, rain, or cold. An insulating layer of water- and sweat-wicking fabric (polyester, neoprene, Capilene, or other synthetic fiber) is best for a basic layer. These fabrics wick sweat away from your body and keep you warm. On hot days cotton can be a good choice only because the sweat will remain on the fabric, keeping you cooler than a synthetic material. Cotton is a bad choice for cold and rainy days, since the material retains water and loses its ability to insulate, which in extreme circumstances can lead to hypothermia.

A fleece shell is good for an insulating layer, because the material is lightweight and dries quickly. On days without a hint of precipitation, a fleece jacket may be the only outerwear needed.

Lastly, a lightweight rain shell should be brought along in case of emergencies. Rain and snow can be deadly in the mountains. A waterproof shell and pants offer protection from the elements.

Improvements in lightweight hiking boots and shoes over the past decade have revolutionized the sport. Boots no longer need to be bulky, heavy, cumbersome, Frankenstein-like appendages that cause blisters, chafing, and sore feet. Instead, many outdoor specialty shops can measure a hiker's feet and find a great-fitting shoe that can be worn immediately on the trail. These shoes are durable and sturdy and are excellent for short day hikes, though they may not be ideal for longer and more difficult trekking.

Socks made of wool or synthetic materials are best, as they pull moisture away from the feet, reducing chafing and blisters.

Backpacks for day hiking should be small, fit comfortably, and carry 10 to 20 pounds. Carrying more than 20 pounds on a day hike is actually kind of silly, and will probably only serve to make the experience less enjoyable. In today's ultralight market, weeklong backpacking trips can be made carrying only 20 to 25 pounds (water and food included), so find a backpack that is large enough to carry what is needed but light enough to be comfortable. Hydration systems have become the norm, and drinking from a reservoir tube is pure bliss compared to the days of cumbersome canteens or stopping to retrieve water bottles from a pack when thirsty.

Trail Regulations/Restrictions

Trails in this guide are located in preserves, and local and regional parks. Some trails pass through private property. As of this writing, access is allowed in these areas, but care should be taken not to abuse this privilege. Be careful and courteous, and always respect private property. Landowners can shut off access to their property if unsightly trash and negative behaviors become the norm. Do your part to protect these refuges.

Some city parks and natural areas are free, while others require day-use fees. Fees for trailhead usage are not required anywhere, though camping permits may carry fees.

Play It Safe

Generally, hiking in and around the South Bay is a safe and fun way to explore the outdoors. Hiking is not without its risks, but there are ways to lessen those risks. Following a few simple steps and guidelines will help to make the activity as benign as possible.

It is a good idea to know simple first aid, including how to treat bleeding, bites and stings, and fractures, strains, or sprains. Be sure to take along at least a basic first-aid kit. It won't help to have the skills without any supplies.

The South Bay, and all of Southern California for that matter, is known for its sunny skies and warm climate. The sun can be powerful, especially at higher elevations; use sunscreen and wear a wide-brimmed hat. Weather patterns can change abruptly. Carry the proper layers of clothing to protect you from temperature changes and rain.

Rattlesnakes may be found on any of the hikes described, particularly from early spring to midfall. Be careful where you place your hands and feet.

Learn how to spot and identify poison oak. Its appearance will change throughout the year. During spring and summer, the distinctive three-pronged leaf may appear green and then turn to red and brown as the season progresses into winter. In winter, the leaves may completely fall off the plant, leaving a hard-to-identify stalk that still contains and spreads the toxins when touched. The noxious plant grows abundantly near water, in the canyons, and along the hillsides.

Ticks are another pest to be avoided. They are more likely to be found near water or after rains, and hang in the brush waiting to drop on warm-blooded animals. It is a good idea to check for ticks whenever pausing along the trail. Ticks will generally hang on to clothing or hair and not bite until the host has stopped moving. Remove them before they have a chance to bite.

Zero Impact

Trails in the South Bay area are heavily used year-round. We, as trail users and advocates, must be especially vigilant to make sure our passage leaves no lasting mark. Here are some basic guidelines for preserving trails in the region:

Pack out all your own trash, including biodegradable items like orange peels and sunflower seeds. In the arid Southern California climate, items such as these take ten or more years to decompose. If everyone who hiked these trails left peels and shells behind, the trails would look more like a waste dump than a forest or wild landscape. You might also pack out garbage left by less considerate hikers—take a plastic bag and make the place better for your having been there.

Don't approach or feed any wild creatures—the ground squirrel eyeing your snack food is best able to survive if it remains self-reliant.

Don't pick wildflowers or gather rocks, antlers, feathers, or other treasures along the trail. Removing these items will only take away from the next hiker's experience.

Avoid damaging trailside soils and plants by remaining on the established route. This is also a good rule of thumb for avoiding poison oak and stinging nettle, common regional trailside irritants.

Don't cut switchbacks, which can promote erosion.

Be courteous by not making loud noises while hiking.

Many of these trails are multiuse, which means you'll share them with other hikers, trail runners, mountain bikers, and equestrians. Familiarize yourself with the proper trail etiquette, yielding the trail when appropriate.

Use outhouses at trailheads or along the trail.

Be respectful of private property rights.

The Falcon Zero-Impact Principles

- Leave with everything you brought with you.
- Leave no sign of your visit.
- Leave the landscape as you found it.

Map Legend

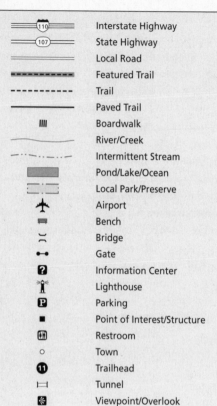

═══⟨110⟩═══	Interstate Highway
───⟨107⟩───	State Highway
═════════	Local Road
▬▬▬▬▬▬	Featured Trail
----------	Trail
──────────	Paved Trail
ⅠⅠⅠⅠ	Boardwalk
～～～	River/Creek
─ ·· ─ ·· ─	Intermittent Stream
▬▬▬	Pond/Lake/Ocean
▭▭▭	Local Park/Preserve
✈	Airport
▭	Bench
⌣	Bridge
•—•	Gate
❓	Information Center
⊼	Lighthouse
🅿	Parking
▪	Point of Interest/Structure
🚻	Restroom
○	Town
⓫	Trailhead
⊢⊣	Tunnel
▨	Viewpoint/Overlook

Beaches

The beaches of the South Bay are world renowned, and are top tourist destinations in their own right. Urban and at times gritty, the beaches have a strange appeal. Each community gives off a different vibe, but the balance of nature, population, and the bizarre create an overpowering vortex for those looking to exercise and stretch their feet on Southern California's sunny shore.

Although it is impossible to find solitude, serenity is everywhere. The Pacific Ocean calmly washes in wave after wave, while the constant hum of the city and its inhabitants produces a white noise that at any moment can be switched off, allowing the Zen-like hum to disappear into the background and making the lovely beachfront surroundings and the exercised heartbeat the only things worth focusing on. However, the shopping, eating, people-watching, and general atmosphere of most of these beaches are some of the nation's finest.

1 Santa Monica Pier and Beach

Take a walk along the lovely Santa Monica Pier, then turn onto the walking and bike path that stretches from Pacific Palisades in the north to Marina del Rey in the south. Enjoy the surprisingly serene atmosphere.

Distance: 3.75 miles out and back

Approximate hiking time: 2 hours

Elevation gain: 50 feet

Trail surface: Pavement, wood, and sand

Best season: Year-round

Other trail users: Joggers, dogs, bicyclists, skateboarders, in-line skaters

Canine compatibility: Leashed dogs permitted

Fees and permits: Parking fee

Maps: USGS Beverly Hills, CA TOPO CD 9 and 10

Contact: City of Santa Monica, Santa Monica Convention and Visitors Bureau; 520 Broadway, Santa Monica, CA 90401; (310) 319-6263, (800) 544-5319; www.santamonica.com

Finding the trailhead: From the interchange of I-405 and I-110, head north on I-405 and drive 16.4 miles. Take exit 53B onto I-10 toward Santa Monica and drive 3.8 miles. Take exit 1A toward Fourth Street. Drive 0.1 mile and turn right onto Colorado Avenue. Park in the structure at Colorado and Second. If full, turn down Second Street and park in the next available lot. GPS coordinates: N34 00.723' / W118 29.645'

The Hike

Santa Monica is home to many great attractions, not the least of which is the amazing pier dominated by a roller coaster and Ferris wheel. Its beach is simple, tourist lined, and filled with sunbathers and exercise enthusiasts. While not specifically designed for people-watching like its neighbor to the south, Venice Beach, Santa Monica Beach provides ample opportunities to see real California eccentrics and much in the way of unconventional behavior. Fantastic shopping and eating experiences also await those who venture onto the Promenade at Third Street.

From the parking structure on Second Street, turn right onto Colorado Avenue and follow it southwest toward the beach and pier. The road narrows and eventually becomes a part of the pier itself. Walk out to the end and explore the shops, arcades, and amusement area, enjoying the surf and sun atmosphere that permeates everywhere. Views of the ocean and the surrounding area abound—enjoy them and head back toward land.

Head toward the southeast side of the pier, and take the steps that descend to the Ocean Front Walk—an enormous paved walkway filled with bicyclists, strollers, joggers, in-line skaters, and every type of person imaginable. From here turn right and walk toward the ocean, getting on the smaller walking and bike path, also paved, which travels more through the middle of the beach.

Follow the path away from the pier southeast toward Venice. Here, though not truly escaped from the cacophony of freeways and hordes of humans, the serenity of the ocean should take over. It won't even matter that there are people everywhere. It is impossible not to break away and just feel the peace of the great Pacific Ocean.

After 2 miles of walking, turn around just after passing a huge parking lot on the right. It is possible to continue all the way through Venice Beach and into Marina del Rey.

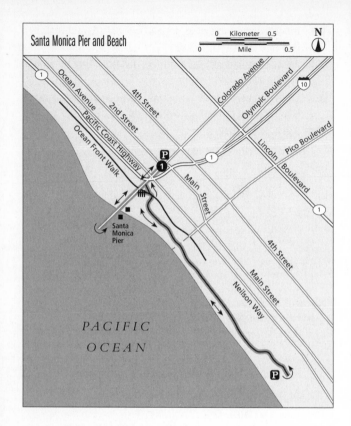

Santa Monica Pier and Beach

PACIFIC
OCEAN

Miles and Directions

0.0 Head southwest from the parking area toward the beach.

0.25 Arrive at the beginning of the pier and walk to the end.

0.5 Arrive at end of pier. Turn around to return to land.

0.75 Veer right and descend stairs to the Ocean Front Walk.

0.8 Turn right onto a smaller trail toward the ocean.

0.9 Turn left and follow the walking and bike path toward Venice Beach.

2.0 After a large parking lot, turn around and head back to the parking area.

3.25 Cross the stream. There is a bridge, but at times the stream is dry and you can walk across the bed.

3.75 Return to the parking area.

2 Venice Beach

Walk along the ocean, enjoying sand and shops. Experience a one-of-a-kind oddity unlike anything else in the world—Venice Beach.

Distance: 3.5 miles out and back
Approximate hiking time: 2 hours
Trail surface: Pavement and sand
Best season: Year-round
Other trail users: Joggers, strollers, wheelchairs, bicyclists, dogs, in-line skaters, skateboarders, roller skaters, eccentrics
Canine compatibility: Leashed dogs permitted

Fees and permits: Parking fees vary throughout the year
Maps: USGS Venice, CA TOPO CD 10
Contact: City of Los Angeles Department of Recreation and Parks, Venice Beach, 1800 Ocean Front Walk, Venice, CA 90291; (323) 644-6661; www .laparks.org/venice/venice.htm

Finding the trailhead: From the interchange of I-405 and I-110, head northwest on I-405 for 12.9 miles. Exit onto CA 90 toward Marina del Rey. Drive 3.2 miles and turn right onto Lincoln Boulevard/CA 1. Turn left onto Washington Boulevard and drive 1.3 miles to the beach. Park in the lot at the beach. GPS coordinates: N33 58.738' / W118 28.036'

The Hike

Venice Beach is a wacky and wild place, renowned for its "board" walk and circus sideshow atmosphere. People of all types walk up and down the boardwalk, from street performer to the just plain bizarre. Visitors to the region can shop, people-watch, or hang out on the sand. The walking and bike path is a great place to put feet to pavement, in-line skate, or ride a bicycle. Food options range from the simplest of fare to the ultra-expensive. It is a good idea to spend several hours here—some of them walking, some of them relaxing, some of them eating, and some of them just witnessing the spectacle.

From the parking area, walk southwest toward the beach and out to the end of the Venice Fishing Pier. The pier is easily recognizable as a location used in various movies and television shows. Enjoy the views of the ocean, Santa Monica Bay, and the islands. Turn around and walk back to the parking area, turning left onto the Ocean Front Walk. Walk north up the wide street (closed to vehicular traffic). This is where the real Venice Beach begins. Here visitors will encounter shopping, murals, artwork, "Muscle Beach," and a host of assorted oddities. Street performers range from amateurish to downright spectacular. Artists regularly create new works as onlookers watch, while graffiti artists, with permission, decorate the murals in the area.

The shops and crowds tend to dwindle beyond Rose Avenue, and just beyond Navy Street the Ocean Front Walk joins up with the walking and bicycle path. Turn left and walk south along this path back to the parking area. Visitors may also choose to walk along the sand and enjoy

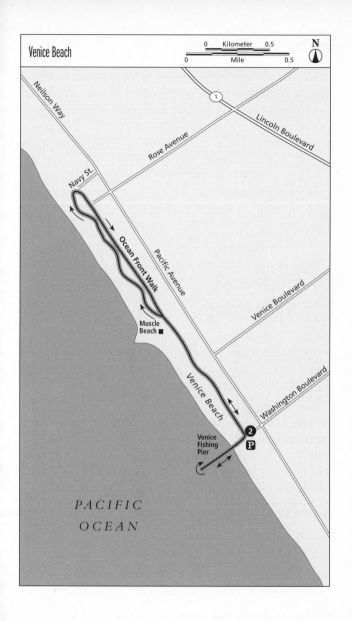

Venice Beach

Neilson Way

1

Rose Avenue

Lincoln Boulevard

Navy St.

Ocean Front Walk

Pacific Avenue

Venice Boulevard

Muscle Beach

Venice Beach

Washington Boulevard

2

P

Venice
Fishing
Pier

PACIFIC

OCEAN

0   Kilometer   0.5

0   Mile   0.5

N

this lovely stretch of Southern California shoreline. There really isn't a wrong way to experience Venice Beach.

Miles and Directions

0.0 Head south from the parking area toward the Venice Fishing Pier.

0.25 Arrive at the end of the pier. Turn around and head back.

0.5 Turn left and walk north along the Ocean Front Walk.

1.0 Arrive at Muscle Beach.

1.9 Arrive at Navy Street. Turn left onto the walking and bike path and return south to the parking lot.

3.5 Return to the parking area.

3 Marina Walk

Walk along the lovely channel at Marina del Rey. Enjoy the ocean views, and explore some of the last remaining sections of the Venice Grand Canal.

Distance: 3 miles out and back
Approximate hiking time: 1.5 hours
Trail surface: Pavement and packed dirt
Best season: Year-round
Other trail users: Dogs, joggers
Canine compatibility: Leashed dogs permitted

Fees and permits: None
Maps: USGS Venice, CA TOPO CD 10
Contact: Marina del Rey Visitors Center, 4701 Admiralty Way, Marina del Rey, CA 90292; (310) 305 9545; www.visit marinadelrey.com

Finding the trailhead: From the interchange of I-405 and I-110, take I-405 north for 12.9 miles. Exit onto CA 90 toward Marina del Rey. Turn right onto Lincoln Boulevard/CA 1 and drive 0.5 mile. Turn left onto Washington Boulevard and drive 0.9 mile. Turn left onto Via Marina and drive 1.2 miles. Turn right to stay on Via Marina and park in the waterfront parking area. Parking spots are metered. GPS coordinates: N33 58.003' / W118 27.233'

The Hike

Marina del Rey is a beautiful, shining gem of the Southern California landscape, charming and idyllic. The peaceful marina and the remnants of the old Venice canals provide abundant opportunities for exploration with much to do and enjoy. Young and old alike will marvel at the waterfowl that reside in and around the canals. The architecture is lovely, and the passing sight of sailboats heading out from the main channel into the great blue of the Pacific should be enough to make anyone happy.

The hike starts near Aubrey E. Austin Park, a tiny green patch on the edge of the water lined with benches for those who wish to watch the passing boats. Walk inland and follow the paved Channel Walk for 0.3 mile. Visitors wishing to further explore the marina, its boats, and the waterway may continue, but here the hike turns around and heads toward the water. Follow the path westward out toward the jetty. The pavement continues nearly to the end.

After enjoying the ocean, some seagoing vessels, and the jetty wall, turn around again and walk 0.3 mile back toward the Grand Canal. Here what is left of old Venice remains. Enter through the gated walkway on either side of the canal and walk along the lovely waterway, enjoying the area's

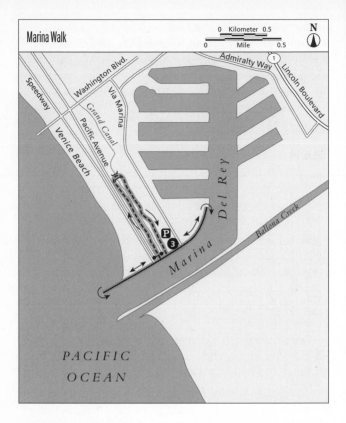

0   Kilometer   0.5

0   Mile   0.5

N

Admiralty Way

Lincoln Boulevard

Speedway

Washington Blvd.

Via Marina

Grand Canal

Pacific Avenue

Venice Beach

Del Rey

Ballona Creek

P

3

Marina

PACIFIC
OCEAN

architecture and serenity. Although many people enjoy the solace of its shores, the walkway is not overcrowded. The canals can be further explored, and the substantial quiet of the waterway is a tangible and gentle reprieve from the otherworldly atmosphere of the beach.

Here the canals of old Venice constructed in 1904 by Abbot Kinney are few and far between. Kinney's vision of an American city resembling Venice, Italy, proved to be impractical in the age of automobiles, and most of the canals were buried by the 1930s and built over. Today that which has been left behind is an upscale neighborhood and a beautiful walkway existing for the enjoyment of those who seek it out.

Miles and Directions

0.0 From the parking area along Via Marina, head east on the Channel Walk inland.

0.3 Turn around and walk west toward the ocean and jetty.

1.3 Arrive at the end of the jetty walkway. Turn around and walk back toward the Grand Canal.

1.7 Turn left and go through the gate. Walk along the Grand Canal.

2.3 Cross the bridge over the canal.

2.9 Turn left onto Via Marina.

3.0 Return to the parking area.

4 Ballona Wetlands

Hike through the largest remaining coastal wetland in the Los Angeles region.

Distance: 3 miles out and back
Approximate hiking time: 1.5 hours
Trail surface: Packed dirt
Best season: Year-round
Other trail users: None
Canine compatibility: No dogs allowed
Fees and permits: None

Maps: USGS Venice, CA TOPO CD 10
Contacts: Friends of Ballona Wetlands, P.O. Box 5159, Playa del Rey, CA 90293; (310) 306-5994; www.ballonafriends.org. Ballona Wetlands Land Trust, P.O. Box 5623, Playa del Rey, CA 90296; (310) 264-9468; www.ballona.org.

Finding the trailhead: From the interchange of I-110 and I-405, take I-405 north for 12.4 miles. Exit onto CA 90 toward Marina del Rey and drive 2.1 miles. Exit at Culver Boulevard, turn left, and drive 1.2 miles. Turn left onto Jefferson Boulevard and park along the eastbound roadway. GPS coordinates: N33 58.194' / W118 26.090'

The Hike

This hike comprises two short trips in the Ballona Wetlands, one of the last surviving significant wetlands in Los Angeles County. Once the wetland area stretched from West Los Angeles to Marina del Rey, but over the course of the twentieth century, Ballona Creek was contained in a concrete flood channel and much of the surrounding land was developed. Since the 1990s various groups have been striving to gain ownership and stop development on what is left of this critical marine and avian habitat.

The beauty of this hike is understated. Two major roadways run beside the property, and CA 90 also drones and howls to the west. Construction and restoration is almost a constant and continuous process, meaning mechanized cranes, backhoes, and storage containers are generally an ever-present sight along the walk. However, this should not deter anyone from exploring the wetlands. The idea is to think of what once was and what could be.

Most of the conservation groups have a similar mindset: expand the parkland and re-create the saltwater marsh, and restore the freshwater marsh, the riparian corridor, the bluffs, and the dunes. Walking through the region, visitors can experience the beauty of this land. Wildlife still abounds, and the sounds of wetland birds continue to resonate above the roar of automobiles. It is quite a lovely atmosphere despite the distractions. The reserve is changing and growing; those interests involved in the protection of Ballona Wetlands have made it a priority to acquire new lands and restore them to their original beauty.

From the parking area on Jefferson, enter the wetlands on the hard dirt path that parallels the roadway. Turn right when nearing Lincoln Boulevard, and follow the trail as it hooks around. Eventually the path will loop around this part of the estuary, but it is not open as of this writing. Return to where Bluff Creek/Teale Street meets Lincoln Boulevard and carefully cross Lincoln. Walk along the athletic fields and enter the wetlands by the path just west of the parking area. Keeping the Playa Vista soccer field on the right, continue to where the path meets the bluffs and head north on the hard dirt trail. Return via the same route to the parking area, carefully cross Lincoln, and head back to Jefferson.

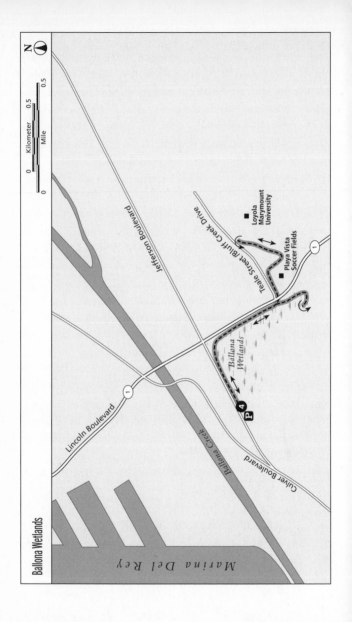

Ballona Wetlands

Marina Del Rey

Lincoln Boulevard

Jefferson Boulevard

Teale Street / Bluff Creek Drive

Loyola Marymount University

Playa Vista Soccer Fields

Ballona Wetlands

Ballona Creek

Culver Boulevard

P 4

1

N

0   Kilometer   0.5

0   Mile   0.5

Miles and Directions

0.0 Enter the preserve on the trail paralleling Jefferson Boulevard and head northwest toward Lincoln Boulevard.

0.3 Turn right and follow the trail as it hooks around the marsh.

0.6 Notice Bluff Creek/Teale Street on the west side of Lincoln.

1.0 Carefully cross Lincoln and walk up Bluff Creek/Teale Street past the athletic fields.

1.3 Turn right and walk south on the path past the soccer field.

1.5 Turn left and walk along the bluffs.

1.8 Reach the end of the trail, turn around, and return to Lincoln Boulevard.

2.6 Cross Lincoln, turn right, and return to the parking area on Jefferson.

3.0 Arrive at the parking area.

5 Del Rey Lagoon

Hike beside a lovely lagoon and enjoy a solitary beach with expansive views of the Ballona Wetlands.

Distance: 1-mile loop
Approximate hiking time: 0.5 hour
Trail surface: Packed dirt and sand
Best season: Year-round
Other trail users: Dogs, joggers
Canine compatibility: Leashed dogs permitted
Fees and permits: None

Maps: USGS Venice, CA TOPO CD 10
Contact: City of Los Angeles Department of Recreation and Parks, Del Rey Lagoon, 6660 Esplanade Place, Playa del Rey, CA 90293; (310) 396-1615; www.laparks.org/dos/aquatic/facility/delreylagoon.htm

Finding the trailhead: From the interchange of I-110 and I-405, drive north on I-405 for 7.5 miles. Exit onto I-105/Imperial Highway west toward El Segundo and drive 4.9 miles. Turn right onto Vista del Mar Avenue and drive 2.1 miles. Turn left onto Culver Boulevard, turn immediately right onto Esplanade Street, and drive 0.1 mile to the parking lot. GPS coordinates: N33 57.562' / W118 27.002'

The Hike

From the parking area, walk north along the lagoon. Sure, this is a fairly residential area close to Los Angeles International Airport (LAX), but most users will find the peaceful calm of Playa del Rey a significant and welcome change from the hustle and bustle of other regions in the Los Angeles metropolitan area. The lagoon is a remnant of the Ballona Creek marshlands, and many migrating birds remain. Bird-watchers and non-birders alike will delight in the avian wildlife here.

As hikers near the end of the lagoon, there is a variety of options. Turning right leads up Ballona Creek, through lands that may eventually be restored to wetland habitat. Making a quick left and crossing over Ballona Creek leads to a bike path atop the concrete channel that separates the creek from the entrance to Marina del Rey. This path also leads past lands that will hopefully be slated for preservation rather than development. Walkers can also choose to head to the end of the south jetty. The featured route, however, leads to the beach.

This section of Dockweiler Beach is hardly ever crowded. It is a great place to relax and just watch the boats entering and leaving the marina. Head back to the lagoon or further explore the beach.

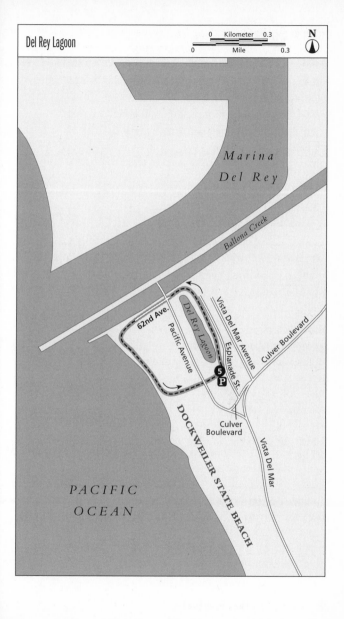

Del Rey Lagoon

0 Kilometer 0.3
0 Mile 0.3

N

Marina Del Rey

Ballona Creek

Del Rey Lagoon

62nd Ave.

Pacific Avenue

Vista Del Mar Avenue

Esplanade St.

Culver Boulevard

5 P

Culver Boulevard

Vista Del Mar

DOCKWEILER STATE BEACH

PACIFIC OCEAN

Miles and Directions

0.0 From the parking area, walk north along the lagoon.

0.3 Turn left and walk through the parking lot or along 62nd Avenue toward the ocean.

0.6 Reach the beach. Walk south and explore the coast.

0.9 Turn left and head back to the parking area.

1.0 Return to the parking area.

6 Dockweiler State Beach

Experience the otherworldly thunder of LAX and explore a beach that seems to be more of a curiosity than any other in the Southland.

Distance: 2 miles out and back
Approximate hiking time: 2 hours
Trail surface: Sand
Best season: Year-round
Other trail users: Bicyclists, in-line skaters, joggers, RV enthusiasts
Canine compatibility: No dogs allowed

Fees and permits: Beach parking lot fee
Maps: USGS Venice, CA Topo CD 10
Contact: LA County Department of Beaches and Harbors, 12000 Vista del Mar, Playa del Rey, CA 90293 (310) 305-9546; www.parks.ca.gov/?page_id=617

Finding the trailhead: From the interchange of I-110 and I-405, take I-405 north for 7.5 miles. Exit onto I-105/Imperial Highway west toward El Segundo and drive 4.9 miles. Turn right onto Vista del Mar Avenue. Parking along the western side of Vista del Mar Avenue is free and plentiful. GPS coordinates: N33 56.226' / W118.26.348'

The Hike

Dockweiler State Beach is definitely an oddity in a land of peculiarity. People call Dockweiler a "city person's" beach, although everyone is almost always friendly and patrol vehicles frequent the shores, making the beach feel safer than many. There is ample free parking along the roadway, but some people still opt to pay for parking access. This may make the beach much more accessible for the less affluent and families.

The views, however, are nothing to write home about. There are the towers and colossal processing centers at the El Segundo Water Treatment Plant, affectionately called "Smellsegundo" by the locals and frequent visitors to the beach. Sometimes when the wind is right, the air can be described as "foul-smelling," but mostly it is okay. Then there are the large tankers that dock just outside the bay—most people do not find them very alluring.

There are a great many compelling things about Dockweiler, though. First of all, all flights departing from LAX take off directly over the beach. There is something incredibly cool and particularly fascinating about giant machines blasting overhead at what seems like jumping distance. Children are sure to be spellbound, not to mention most adults. It is very easy to spend hours watching the biggest jets soar up into the sky and wonder where they're going. Needless to say, Dockweiler is not the beach to head to for those seeking serenity and quiet.

The bike path here is much more open than in places like Venice or Santa Monica or the beaches farther south. It is a great place to in-line skate and walk along the sand. There are fire pits where those so inclined can barbeque

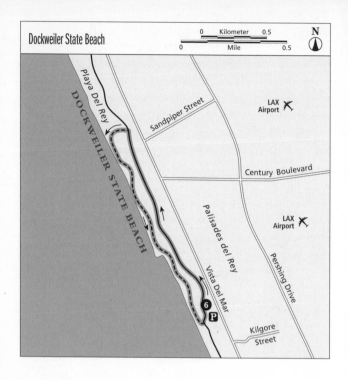

and have bonfires, which is a rarity on Southern California beaches these days.

The last oddity is not something that can be explored, but those driving on Vista del Mar will surely notice the remnant streets of Palisades del Rey, some still landscaped with palms and other trees. The community was designed in the 1920s, with homes being built in the 1950s and '60s. When LAX expanded, the residents opted for a mass buy-out due to noise and perhaps the sheer insanity that can be caused by the constant barrage of jumbo jets. The homes were removed, but curiously the streets remain, and the fenced-off ghost community is now a protected habitat for the endangered El Segundo blue butterfly. The butterfly is quite a unique and pretty specimen—count yourself lucky if you see one.

This hike is more of a do-it-yourself walk on the beach, and any number of routes can be followed along the bike path or shoreline.

Miles and Directions

0.0 From the streetside parking along the west side of Vista del Mar, walk toward the bike path and the ocean.

0.1 Turn north and walk along the bike path.

0.75 Turn west and head south along the shoreline.

1.5 Turn east and head back to parking spot.

2.0 Return to streetside parking.

7 Manhattan to Redondo Beach

Walk along the attractive and renowned Strand from one famous tourist beach to another.

Distance: 5 miles out and back
Approximate hiking time: 2–3 hours
Trail surface: Pavement
Best season: Late fall through early spring. Do not enter slot canyons during rain or times of runoff.
Other trail users: Joggers, in-line skaters, bicyclists
Canine compatibility: Leashed dogs permitted; no dogs on beaches
Fees and permits: Parking fee
Maps: USGS Venice and Redondo Beach, CA TOPO CD 10
Contact: City of Manhattan Beach, 1400 Highland Ave., Manhattan Beach, CA 90266; (310) 802-5000; www.ci.manhattan-beach.ca.us

Finding the trailhead: From the interchange of I-110 and I-405, head north on I-405 for 5 miles to exit 42B, Inglewood Avenue. Turn left onto Inglewood Avenue and drive 0.3 mile. Turn right onto Manhattan Beach Boulevard and drive 2.9 miles to the end of the road and pier parking. GPS coordinates: N33 56.226' / W118.26.348'

The Hike

Manhattan Beach is an ideal Southern California coastal town. Located in the southern part of Los Angeles County, the city is home to high-priced housing, great beachside shopping, surfing, sunbathing, outdoor recreation, and lots of fantastic gastronomic opportunities. The communities of Hermosa Beach and Redondo Beach pretty much fall into the same category as Manhattan, and those walking along the beach will not be able to tell where one town starts and the other one ends. There isn't much in the way of solitude, with the beaches and

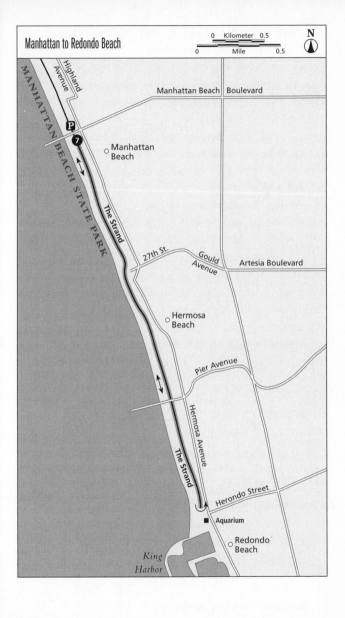

Manhattan to Redondo Beach

N

0   Kilometer   0.5
0   Mile   0.5

MANHATTAN BEACH STATE PARK

Highland Avenue

Manhattan Beach Boulevard

P
7

Manhattan Beach

The Strand

27th St.

Gould Avenue

Artesia Boulevard

Hermosa Beach

Pier Avenue

Hermosa Avenue

The Strand

Herondo Street

Aquarium

Redondo Beach

King Harbor

cities surrounded on all sides by urbanity, freeways, and the constant roar of civilization. However, beach communities in Southern California have always been able to rise above their big-city suburban counterparts and somehow feel more remote, peaceful, and easygoing. These three beach towns are no exception to that rule.

Connecting the three cities is an incredible beach walking and bike path known to locals as "The Strand." Lots of people walk, run, bicycle, and in-line skate along this path. It is not necessarily full of people, but there are always others coming and going in both directions. Obviously, the beach is the main draw here for those looking for outdoor activity, and it provides a powerful backdrop to any action undertaken along the way.

The route here is simple: Head south along the Strand, taking any detour that seems fitting, whether it be a walk on the beach, fun in the sun, a trip through the shopping district, or a stroll on a pier. There is much to do and see in the area, including a free marine exhibit on the Manhattan Pier and a free aquarium at Redondo Beach at Herondo and Hermosa. Those who wish to may continue along the boardwalk at Redondo Beach and inspect the curiosities and shops while checking out the interesting triangular pier. Return to the parking area whenever you like. Just make sure the meter is paid for the duration of the visit—tickets can be pricey.

Miles and Directions

0.0 From the parking lot at the end of Manhattan Avenue, walk south along the Strand.

2.5 Reach Redondo Beach. Turn around and return to the parking area.

5.0 Arrive back at the parking lot.

Palos Verdes Peninsula

Palos verdes means "green sticks" in Spanish, and the peninsula's name was probably derived from the native palo verde tree common to the area. There are many open spaces left on the peninsula, and access is relatively free to most of them.

Luxurious homes dominate much of the region, and equestrian trails abound. Tremendous views of the coast and coastal regions can be had at many different locations, and an escape to a seminatural setting is only minutes away almost anywhere in the area. Although the truly wild may be out of reach, most of these open spaces and parks will leave the visitor satisfied with the opportunity to exercise and enjoy some time in the great outdoors.

The Palos Verdes Peninsula Land Conservancy has purchased quite a bit of land over the past several years. These preserves are dedicated to restoring the land to its original native ecosystems, as it was before the arrival of the Spanish. The conservancy has done a fantastic job of opening these lands to hiking and keeping them beautiful. It has also been highly successful in restoring native habitat critical for the survival of certain endangered species.

8 Madrona Marsh

Stroll through a lovely vernal marsh, experiencing wildlife, nature, and beauty in an urban setting.

Distance: 1-mile figure 8
Approximate hiking time: 1 hour
Trail surface: Packed dirt
Best season: Spring is best, but the preserve is beautiful year-round.
Other trail users: Bird-watchers, strollers, school groups
Canine compatibility: No dogs allowed
Fees and permits: None

Restrictions: Open Tues through Sun 10:00 a.m. to 5:00 p.m.; closed holidays
Maps: USGS Torrance, CA TOPO CD 10
Contact: City of Torrance, Madrona Marsh Preserve and Nature Center, 3201 Plaza del Amo, Torrance, CA 90503; (310) 782-3989; www.fs.fed.us/r5/angeles

Finding the trailhead: From the interchange of I-110 and I-405, head south on I-110 for 1.5 miles. Take the Carson Street exit, turn right onto Carson, and drive 3 miles. Turn left onto Maple Avenue and drive 0.3 mile. Turn right onto Plaza del Amo/Toledo Street and drive 0.2 mile. Parking and visitor center are on the right. GPS coordinates: N33 49.704' / W118 20.531'

The Hike

From the parking lot, stop at the visitor center to get a better understanding of the preserve. Here visitors can explore interactive exhibits and get a sense of the marsh's plants and animals, while also obtaining a better grasp of the history and ecology of the area. There are several hands-on activities that are great for children of all ages. After spending some time getting acquainted with the ecosystem, cross Plaza del Amo and enter the actual preserve.

Walking through the marsh is a fairly easy do-it-yourself experience, though the route described here works out to be a mile's worth of walking. Visitors can take any route they wish, and there is truly no set path or right or wrong way to go. Some visitors will be so enchanted by this strikingly beautiful parcel of land wedged between urban expanse, enormous shopping malls, and apartment complexes that they may wish to loop around several times, exploring all the twists and turns the preserve has to offer. The preserve is fairly small, about the size of a large city block, so it is impossible to get lost, but the place feels surprisingly serene. Feel free to explore and simply let the path lead the way.

The Madrona Marsh is all that is left of what much of Southern California used to look like before cities took over. Vernal marshes used to be common everywhere throughout the Southland. Small depressions would fill after being fed with water from winter rains and spring runoff from snowmelt in the higher mountains, leaving behind swampy grasslands and forests. This parcel was preserved by accident because of oil interests on the property; otherwise, it may have been overrun by housing and land development like nearly every other property in the area.

The preserve has been given a facelift to bring it back to a more natural state. While many of the trees and plants have been planted by volunteers and biologists, the Friends of Madrona Marsh has been working to restore the preserve since 1973. The region is without a doubt lovely. It is little utilized, rarely crowded, and worth the trip. Most visitors to the marsh will want to return season after season and year after year.

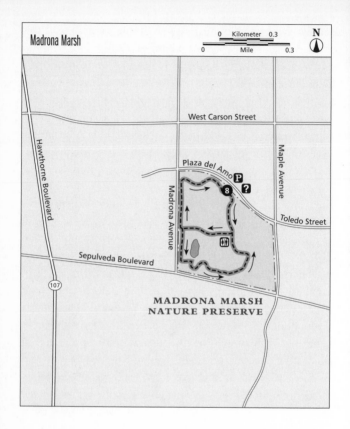

After crossing the road, walk south 500 feet, turn right, and continue into the heart of the preserve. After another 400 feet, turn right at a Y intersection in the middle of the marsh area. Walk another 400 feet and turn left to skirt the perimeter of the park. Follow the trail as it loops around the marshland and nears the restroom. From the restroom, walk 500 feet north to the earlier trail split. Follow the same split, except this time turn right at the edge of the preserve and complete a nearly figure 8 loop around the marsh before returning to the parking area.

Miles and Directions

0.0 From the visitor center, cross Plaza del Amo to the south. Stay on the main trail heading south.

0.2 Turn right before the restroom, heading into the marsh toward the vernal pool.

0.3 Turn left and walk around the perimeter of the park.

0.5 Turn left and loop around the vernal pool.

0.6 Pass the restroom.

0.7 Turn left back into the marshland.

0.8 Turn right at the preserve perimeter.

0.9 Turn right and return to the parking area.

1.0 Arrive back at the visitor center.

9 Malaga Cove

Climb heights to see awe-inspiring views of Malaga Cove, walk through wooded areas, and then descend to the beach.

Distance: 4-mile lollipop
Approximate hiking time: 2 hours
Elevation gain: 800 feet
Trail surface: Packed dirt and pavement
Best season: Year-round
Other trail users: Dogs, joggers
Canine compatibility: Leashed dogs permitted; dogs prohibited on beach

Fees and permits: None
Maps: USGS Redondo Beach, CA TOPO CD 10
Contact: County of Los Angeles Department of Beaches and Harbors, 13837 Fiji Way, Marina del Rey, CA 90292; (310) 305-9503; http://beaches.co.la.ca.us

Finding the trailhead: From the interchange of I-110 and I-405, head south on I-110 for 4 miles. Take exit 4 for Pacific Coast Highway/CA 1 and turn right. Drive 3 miles and turn left onto Crenshaw Boulevard. Drive 1.3 miles and turn right onto Palos Verdes Drive North. Drive 2.9 miles and make a slight left onto Palos Verdes Drive West. Drive 0.1 mile and turn left onto Via Chico. Turn immediately right onto Via Tejon and park in the Malaga Cove Plaza. GPS coordinates: N33 48.006' / W118 23.400'

The Hike

This hike takes streets and dirt paths through public-access areas in Palos Verdes. Park in the Malaga Cove Plaza parking lot, where a re-creation of the famous Fontana del Nettuno (Neptune's Fountain) in Bologna, Italy, stands and impresses visitors to the shopping mall. From here, walk east up Via Tejon to the end of the road and follow the trail up through the dirt. At 0.4 mile turn right and head up through the dry creek bed, climbing the canyon under shady trees paralleling the edge of the golf course at the Palos Verdes Country Club.

Tremendous views of the cove can be had along many parts of the trail, and the route feels surprisingly wild in most areas that are not along the street. Wildlife can be seen, and the hike is mostly shady and pleasant.

At 0.6 mile the route passes beneath Via Campesina through a tunnel and connects with a paved trail. Turn right and follow the pavement as it becomes Paseo del Sol. At 1.5 miles the road connects with Via del Monte; turn right and walk down the road for 0.15 mile, then turn right onto Via Solomonte. Turn left onto Via Conejo, make a quick right onto Via del Monte, and a quick left onto Via Montemar. Make a right onto Via Lazo and the next right onto Via Arriba. To the left is a stairwell that leads down to a trail. Turn right and follow it back through the wash to the Malaga Cove Plaza. Just before returning to the plaza, turn left onto Via Corta. Walk along the sidewalk to where the road becomes Via Almar. Follow the use path beyond the baseball diamonds, through the wash, and down to the cove.

Return to the plaza and the parking area via the same route.

Miles and Directions

0.0 Head east along Via Tejon Place to the end of the road.

0.2 Continue east up the hill.

0.4 Turn right and hike up a wash.

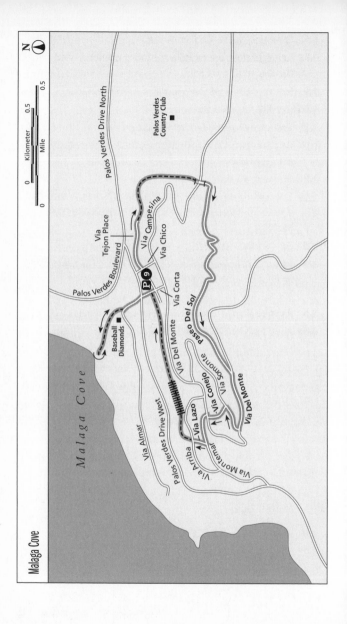

Malaga Cove

Malaga Cove

N

0   Kilometer   0.5

0   Mile   0.5

Palos Verdes Drive North

Palos Verdes Country Club

Via Tejon Place

Via Campesina

Via Chico

Palos Verdes Boulevard

P 9

Via Corta

Via Del Monte

Paseo Del Sol

Baseball Diamonds

Via Somonte

Via Conejo

Via Del Monte

Via Almar

Palos Verdes Drive West

Via Lazo

Via Arriba

Via Montemar

0.6 Cross underneath Via Campesina.

0.75 Turn right along the paved access road and follow it as it becomes Paseo del Sol.

1.5 Turn right at the intersection with Via del Monte.

1.65 Turn right onto Via Somonte.

1.85 Turn left and head north on Via Conejo.

1.9 Turn right onto Via del Monte, then make an immediate left onto Via Montemar.

2.1 Turn right onto Via Lazo.

2.15 Turn right onto Via Arriba. Look for the stairs on the left; descend to a trail and follow it back toward Malaga Cove Plaza.

2.8 Turn left onto Via Corta.

3.0 As Via Corta curves and turns into Via Almar, follow the use trail beside the baseball diamonds. Continue toward the beach.

3.5 Arrive at Malaga Cove. Return via the same route.

4.0 Arrive back at Malaga Cove Plaza.

10 Ernie J. Howlett Park–Telephone Pole Loop

Take horse trails and easements between houses and undeveloped land, gaining commanding views of the Southland and experiencing the outdoors in a quiet neighborhood.

Distance: 4-mile loop
Approximate hiking time: 2 hours
Elevation gain: 300 feet
Trail surface: Packed dirt and asphalt
Best season: Year-round
Other trail users: Dogs, bicycles, horses
Canine compatibility: Leashed

dogs permitted
Fees and permits: None
Maps: USGS Torrance, CA TOPO CD 10
Contact: City of Rancho Palos Verdes, 30940 Hawthorne Blvd., Rancho Palos Verdes, CA 90275; (310) 377-0360; www.palos verdes.com/rpv

Finding the trailhead: From the interchange of I-110 and I-405, take I-110 south for 4.4 miles. Take exit 4 for Pacific Coast Highway/ CA 1 and turn right. Drive 3 miles and turn left onto Crenshaw Boulevard. Drive 0.5 mile and make a right onto Rolling Hills Road. Drive 0.7 mile and turn left onto Hawthorne Boulevard. Drive 0.4 mile and turn right into the parking area by the baseball diamonds. GPS coordinates: N33 47.591' / W118 21.190'

The Hike

This hike utilizes some of the horse trails, access ways, alleys, and easements that snake their way through the community of Palos Verdes. The well-used network of paths has become a property rights and liability issue for the city and home owners in the area, so be careful and respectful when traveling any of these routes. Most of the hiking is between houses and private property, but the route is tree-lined and shaded and feels outright natural. It is actually part of an informal network of paths and trails. Remember that in some places the right to travel may be revoked at any time; it is always wise to value the places where the public has been granted access.

Start at the Ernie J. Howlett Park parking lot. Walk to the west of the baseball fields, and take the equestrian trail south and west from the stables. Walk along the trail for 0.5 mile. Here the dirt trail crosses Masongate Drive and continues west for another 0.25 mile until reaching Palos Verdes Drive North. Turn right and make an immediate left onto Via Campesina. Less than 100 feet from the intersection an easement between houses continues on the right; follow it north. In less than 0.1 mile the trail crosses Via Palomino, and in another 0.15 mile it crosses Via Valmonte.

Here the route begins to turn westward, crossing Via Navajo and Via Colusa. Follow Via Colusa 0.1 mile to the telephone pole in the center of the street, marking this as the unofficial "telephone pole trail." Turn right and follow the access corridor unimpeded by crossings for 0.75 mile. Curve right at the fork and follow the smaller access trail up a hill. Make a left onto Via Nivel and walk 0.15 mile to Via Valmonte. Cross the street and follow the small unmarked trail behind the NOT A THROUGH STREET sign. Make a left onto Via Pinzon and follow it to its end. Walk through the open space up a hill, take in the outstanding views, and continue along the ledge back to Ernie J. Howlett Park.

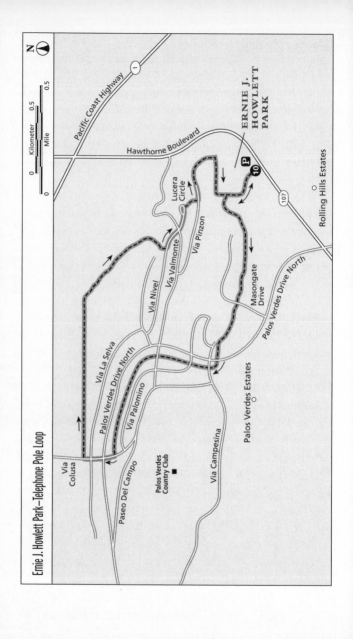

Ernie J. Howlett Park–Telephone Pole Loop

Miles and Directions

0.0 From the parking lot, walk west behind the baseball fields to the horse trail by the stables.

0.6 Cross Masongate Drive and continue west.

0.9 Turn right onto Palos Verdes Drive North, then make an immediate left onto Via Campesina.

0.95 Turn right onto the access trail between houses.

1.0 Cross Via Palomino and head north.

1.2 Cross Via Valmonte and continue north.

1.5 Cross Via Navajo and head west.

1.75 Turn right onto Via Colusa.

1.8 Cross Palos Verdes Drive North.

1.85 Cross Via La Selva and continue to where the road stops at the telephone pole. Turn right onto the easement and follow it eastward.

3.0 Turn right at the fork in the wooded canyon.

3.2 Turn left onto Via Nivel.

3.3 Cross Via Valmonte toward Lucera Circle; take the small trail behind the NOT A THROUGH STREET sign.

3.4 Turn left onto Via Pinzon and follow it to its end.

3.6 Continue east along the access trail through the open lot along the hillside. Follow it back to Ernie J. Howlett Park and the parking area.

4.0 Return to the parking area.

11 South Coast Botanic Garden

Enjoy a stroll through the South Bay's beautiful Botanic Garden. Visit lovely collections, watch for birds, and take detours along peaceful side paths.

Distance: 1.3-mile loop
Approximate hiking time: 1 hour
Elevation gain: 100 feet
Trail surface: Pavement
Best season: Spring is prettiest, but the gardens are nice year-round.
Other trail users: Bird-watchers, strollers, tour groups
Canine compatibility: No dogs allowed

Fees and permits: Admission fee
Restrictions: Open daily 9:00 a.m. to 5:00 p.m.; closed Christmas
Maps: USGS Torrance, CA TOPO CD 10
Contact: South Coast Botanic Garden, 26300 Crenshaw Blvd., Palos Verdes Peninsula, CA 90274; (310) 544-1948; www .southcoastbotanicgarden.org

Finding the trailhead: From the interchange of I-110 and I-405, head south on I-110 for 4.4 miles. Take exit 4 for Pacific Coast Highway/CA 1, turn right, and drive 3 miles. Turn left onto Crenshaw Boulevard and drive 1 mile. Turn left into the parking lot. GPS coordinates: N33 46.999' / W118 20.957'

The Hike

The striking South Coast Botanic Garden is a gem of the South Bay. While springtime is obviously the best time for blooms and splendor, the garden always has something to show off, and it is a great place to get out and enjoy nature and all of its beauty any time of year.

Flower gardens such as the fuchsia, rose, and dahlia are spectacular when in full blossom. The Children's Garden was

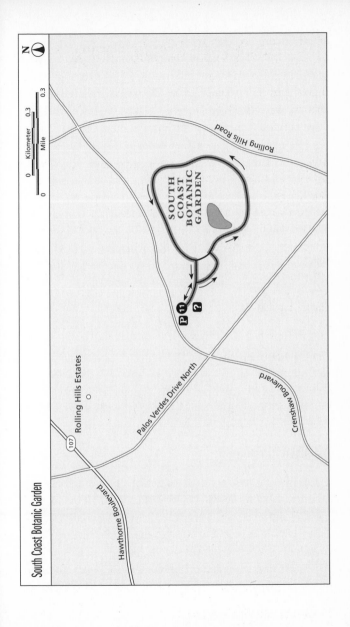

South Coast Botanic Garden

created out of nursery rhyme lore and is definitely a must-see for those hiking with young ones. Interactive gardens such as the Garden for the Senses offer an experience through smell, touch, and sight. There are gardens to delight almost any taste and enough different paths to take around the park that visitors can spend many hours just enjoying the walk.

The garden has quite an interesting history. It started off as a mine for diatomaceous earth, a substance used in items ranging from blood-clotting agents to kitty litter. Diatomaceous earth is fossilized algae left over from when the region was covered by the ocean. After the mining operation was finished, the property became a landfill in the 1950s. By 1961 a group of interested citizens persuaded the Los Angeles County Board of Supervisors to turn the area into the botanic garden that exists today, providing a sanctuary for insects and wildlife.

From the parking area, take the southernmost path around the administration buildings and head east along the pathway passing the fuchsia, California natives, and succulents. Join the main road around the gardens at the intersection with the beautiful rose garden, then turn right and follow the loop counterclockwise past redwoods, acacias, conifers, palms, banyans, and a Mediterranean garden before returning to the parking area.

Miles and Directions

- **0.0** Walk to the south side of the parking area and head east beside the administration buildings.
- **0.2** Make a U-shaped turn past the succulent garden to the main road. Turn right and follow the main road counterclockwise around the gardens.
- **1.1** Turn right to return to the parking area.
- **1.3** Return to the parking area.

12 Linden H. Chandler Preserve

Wander through a 28.5-acre property and explore the recently restored wetlands. The parcel serves as habitat for the spectacular Palos Verdes blue butterfly.

Distance: 1-mile loop
Approximate hiking time: 0.5 hour
Elevation gain: 150 feet
Trail surface: Packed dirt and pavement
Best season: Year-round
Other trail users: Dogs, horses, joggers

Canine compatibility: Leashed dogs permitted
Fees and permits: None
Maps: USGS Torrance, CA TOPO CD 10
Contact: Palos Verdes Peninsula Land Conservancy, P.O. Box 3247, Palos Verdes Peninsula, CA 90274; (310) 541-7613; www.pvplc.org

Finding the trailhead: From the interchange of I-110 and I-405, take I-110 south for 4.1 miles to exit 4, Pacific Coast Highway/CA 1. Turn right onto Pacific Coast Highway and drive 0.5 mile. Make a left onto Vermont and drive 0.4 mile. Stay left and continue on Vermont for another 0.4 mile. Vermont becomes Palos Verdes Drive North; drive another 2.1 miles and turn right onto Dapplegray Lane. Make the first left onto Buckskin Lane, drive to the end, and park. GPS coordinates: N33 46.689' / W118 19.934'

The Hike

The Linden H. Chandler Preserve is a peaceful open space full of rolling hills, restored wetlands, and coastal sage scrub. The property was donated in 1994 to the Palos Verdes Peninsula Land Conservancy by the Chandler family and named after its patriarch. The conservancy is working to restore

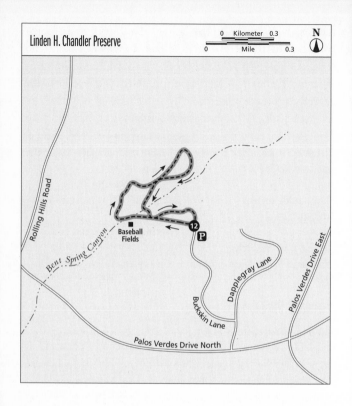

the parcel to its natural condition before the introduction of various nonnative vegetation. Wildlife is also being released into the area, including owls and the beautiful Palos Verdes blue butterfly.

There is no right or wrong way to see the preserve. It may be small in size, but the landscape is beautiful and hikers will get a sense of getting away from it all, despite being very close to the city. To make a 1-mile loop from the parking area on Buckskin Lane, head west along the perimeter of the preserve, straddling the houses that neighbor the parkland. Follow the path 0.25 mile past the baseball fields and make a right, again skirting along the border. An interpretive sign marks the intersection, highlighting some of the natural features of the land.

At 0.4 mile, make a right and follow the short spur on the left to make a loop next to the golf course. At 0.6 mile, continue south and left on the main trail. At 0.7 mile, the trail dips back to the original east–west route from the parking area. Turn left and make an immediate left onto the trail that leads to the middle of the park. Make a series of lefts as many trails cross. The parking lot is not very far away, and hikers can shorten the walk by dropping south back to the lot, or explore the small side canyon on the eastern section of the preserve.

Miles and Directions

0.0 From the end of the road, turn left and head west toward the baseball fields.

0.25 Just beyond the baseball fields, turn right and continue to skirt the border of the park. Reach an interpretive sign that describes some of the features of the area.

0.4 Turn right, then take a left at the Y and follow the small loop next to the golf course. Return to the main trail.

0.6 Turn left and follow the trail through the center of the preserve.

0.7 Turn left onto the trail from the parking area to the baseball fields, then make an immediate left. Make three more lefts over the course of the next 0.2 mile.

0.9 Make a right, and walk toward the parking area.

1.0 Arrive back at the parking area.

13 George F. Canyon Preserve

Hike through a wonderfully secluded preserve on an interpretive trail that leads through a lovely riparian canyon and stream.

Distance: 1.5 miles out and back

Approximate hiking time: 1 hour

Elevation gain: 250 feet

Trail surface: Packed dirt

Best season: Year-round

Other trail users: Horses

Canine compatibility: No dogs allowed

Fees and permits: None

Maps: USGS Torrance, CA TOPO CD 10

Contacts: George F. Canyon Nature Center, 27305 Palos Verdes Dr., East Rolling Hills Estates, CA 90274; (310) 547-0862. Palos Verdes Peninsula Land Conservancy, P.O. Box 3247, Palos Verdes Peninsula, CA 90274; (310) 541-7613; www.pvplc.org.

Finding the trailhead: From the interchange of I-110 and I-405, take I-110 south for 4.1 miles. Take exit 4 for Pacific Coast Highway/CA 1. Turn right onto Pacific Coast Highway and drive 0.5 mile. Make a left onto Vermont and drive 0.4 mile. Stay left and continue on Vermont for another 0.4 mile. Vermont becomes Palos Verdes Drive North; drive another 1.8 miles. Turn left onto Palos Verdes Drive East and turn right into the parking area. GPS coordinates: N33 46.314' / W118 19.612'

The Hike

The George F. Canyon Nature Center sits at the head of one of the loveliest and most unspoiled canyons left in the Palos Verdes region. Despite being sandwiched between housing tracts, the canyon retains a magic and sparkle that generally feels untouched by the hand of humanity.

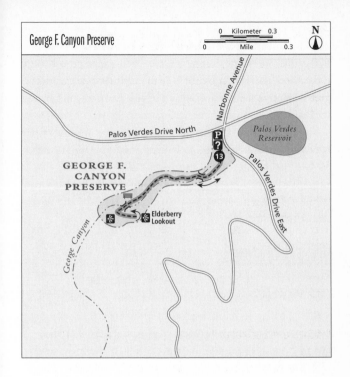

The center sponsors many outreach and educational programs, including docent-led hikes, full moon night hikes, a monthly bird walk, family fun days, and a birthday safari for children age six to twelve. The center itself is set up for education and hands-on activities.

The trail through George F. Canyon Preserve starts behind the nature center and heads south, paralleling Palos Verdes Drive East and passing the sign and dedication monument marking the entrance to the trail. From here twelve interpretive stops marked by posts await hikers as the trail gently climbs to two different lookout points. The interpretive stops describe things to look for, such as birds, raptors, and nonnative plants, and some things to avoid, such as poison oak. The trail crosses the first bridge at 0.2 mile and crosses the second one at the 0.5-mile bench.

From this point the trail continues upward a short way to the raptor-viewing bench, where it is not unusual to see red-tailed hawks and, though less common, various other birds of prey. The route continues a short bit farther to an overlook of the Los Angeles Basin and a view of the nature center. Here, visitors retrace their steps back to the center and parking area.

Miles and Directions

0.0 Head south on the trail behind the nature center.

0.1 Turn right and follow the trail westward.

0.2 Cross a bridge and head up the north side of the creek.

0.5 Pass the 0.5-mile bench and walk across another bridge.

0.75 Reach the Elderberry Lookout. Turn around and return to the parking area.

1.5 Arrive back at the parking area.

14 Point Vicente Park

Visit a historic lighthouse with outstanding views of the coast and the Palos Verdes bluffs.

Distance: 1.6 miles out and back
Approximate hiking time: 1 hour
Trail surface: Packed dirt and pavement
Best season: Year-round
Other trail users: Dogs
Canine compatibility: Leashed dogs permitted
Fees and permits: None

Maps: USGS Redondo Beach OE S, CA TOPO CD 10
Contact: City of Rancho Palos Verdes, Point Vicente Interpretive Center, 31501 Palos Verdes Dr., West Rancho Palos Verdes, CA 90274; (310) 377-5370; www .palosverdes.com/rpv/recreation parks/PointVicenteInterpretive Center

Finding the trailhead: From the interchange of I-405 and I-110, head south on I-110 for 4.1 miles. Take exit 4 for Pacific Coast Highway/CA 1. Turn right onto Pacific Coast Highway and drive 3 miles. Turn left onto Crenshaw Boulevard and drive 3.4 miles. Turn right onto Crest Road and drive 1.6 miles. Turn left onto Hawthorne Boulevard and drive 2.1 miles. Continue straight on Via Vicente/Calle Entradero for 0.2 mile. Park along the street in the parking spaces on the right. GPS coordinates: N33 45.114' / W118.24.734'

The Hike

The Point Vicente Lighthouse is one of the most beautiful, picturesque, and photographed spots along the Palos Verdes Peninsula. The lighthouse itself, operated by the U.S. Coast Guard, is open for tours from 10:00 a.m. to 3:00 p.m. on the second Saturday of every month except March, when it is open on the first Saturday. Nearby to the north is an

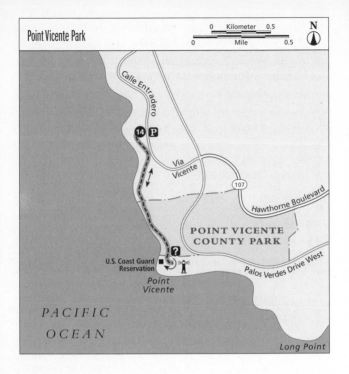

0   Kilometer   0.5

0   Mile   0.5

N

Calle Entradero

14 P

Via Vicente

107

Hawthorne Boulevard

**POINT VICENTE
COUNTY PARK**

?

U.S. Coast Guard
Reservation

*Point
Vicente*

Palos Verdes Drive West

PACIFIC

OCEAN

Long Point

interpretive center where visitors can learn about the natural and cultural history of the peninsula. It makes a good midway stop for this hike.

From the street parking along Calle Entradero, head west toward the bluffs that drop away precipitously to the Pacific Ocean. Turn south and walk along the cliffs, taking in the dramatic views of Santa Catalina Island, the ocean, and the Point Vicente Lighthouse. The spectacular views are breathtaking. Walk south for 0.5 mile and turn inland to the road that leads to the interpretive center.

The center is open daily from 10:00 a.m. to 5:00 p.m. and is a great place to learn about the area and the whales that migrate past it. If visiting during whale season (approximately November through March), it is not uncommon to see them passing by from the point. The center has picnic benches that make for a great snack stop, especially if you have children with you. Continue on to the lighthouse, taking a tour if the timing is right, then return north to the street parking.

Miles and Directions

0.0 Walk west along the trail toward the ocean and bluffs.

0.1 Turn south and walk toward the lighthouse.

0.5 Turn left and inland toward the interpretive center.

0.6 Arrive at the interpretive center.

0.8 Reach the lighthouse gate. Return via the same route.

1.6 Arrive at the parking area.

15 Burma Road Trail

Hike along old Crenshaw Boulevard in what is now Portuguese Bend Preserve. Take in outstanding vistas, and travel through a lovely wooded canyon.

Distance: 2.75-mile lollipop
Approximate hiking time: 1.5 hours
Elevation gain: 560 feet
Trail surface: Packed dirt
Best season: Year-round
Other trail users: Dogs, horses, joggers, bicyclists
Canine compatibility: Leashed dogs permitted
Fees and permits: None
Maps: USGS San Pedro, CA TOPO CD 10
Contact: Palos Verdes Peninsula Land Conservancy, P.O. Box 3247, Palos Verdes Peninsula, CA 90274; (310) 541-7613; www.pvplc.org

Finding the trailhead: To reach Del Cerro Park from the interchange of I-405 and I-110, drive south on I-110 for 4.1 miles. Take exit 4 for Pacific Coast Highway/CA 1. Turn right onto Pacific Coast Highway and drive 3 miles. Turn left onto Crenshaw Boulevard and drive 3.8 miles. Turn right onto Park Place and park in the lot. GPS coordinates: N33 45.465' / W118 22.050'

The Hike

Portuguese Bend Preserve is operated by the Palos Verdes Peninsula Land Conservancy and is one of the largest open spaces in the South Bay. Crisscrossed by trails, the vistas are wide and the canyons deep. Some trails are designated for pedestrians only, while others allow horses and bicyclists. This is a fantastic open space with many different combinations of trails and loops that can be strung together for an outstanding hiking experience.

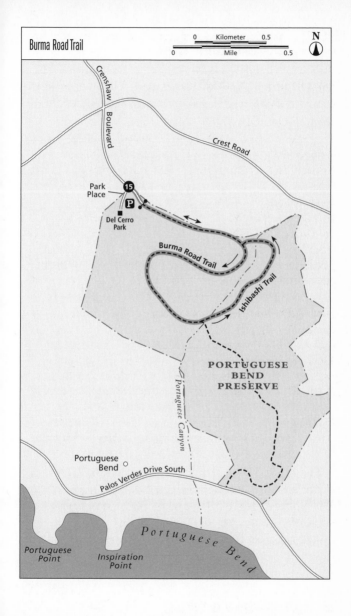

Kilometer

0 0.5

Mile

0 0.5

N

Crenshaw Boulevard

Crest Road

Park Place

15

P

Del Cerro Park

Burma Road Trail

Ishibashi Trail

PORTUGUESE BEND PRESERVE

Portuguese Canyon

Portuguese Bend

Palos Verdes Drive South

Portuguese Bend

Portuguese Point

Inspiration Point

This route combines two trails and starts at Del Cerro Park. The views begin early. From Del Cerro Park, the Pacific panorama extends from the lighthouse at Point Vicente to Long Point along Abalone Cove, through the lovely dual arms into the sea of Portuguese Point and Inspiration Point, and out to Catalina Island. It is truly spectacular, and not a bad spot for sunsets. Hiking just before dusk is a magnificent time to be out along these hillsides.

From the parking at Del Cerro or farther down Crenshaw, walk through the gated lot onto old Crenshaw Boulevard. The road is dirt now and has been renamed the Burma Road Trail. Follow the dirt road as it snakes down the hillside for 1.6 miles. Turn left onto the Ishibashi Trail and head north up the canyon. Hikers can walk just above the canyon or meander through it along a use trail. At the top, turn left and connect back up with Crenshaw Boulevard/Burma Road Trail, returning to the parking area and the tremendous vistas.

Miles and Directions

0.0 From Del Cerro Park, walk east down Crenshaw Boulevard to the gated entrance for Portuguese Bend Preserve.

0.1 Enter the park and continue on the Burma Road Trail. Stay on the road until the second intersection with the Ishibashi Trail.

1.6 Turn left up Portuguese Canyon along the Ishibashi Trail.

2.0 Turn left and connect back up with Crenshaw Boulevard/Burma Road Trail. Stay to the right for the main Burma Road Trail. Retrace your steps.

2.75 Arrive back at the parking area.

16 Klondike Canyon

Walk along a beautiful coastal canyon and meander through the lovely hillsides of Portuguese Bend Preserve.

Distance: 1.5-mile loop
Approximate hiking time: 1 hour
Elevation gain: 400 feet
Trail surface: Packed dirt road and pavement
Best season: Year-round
Other trail users: Dogs, horses, joggers
Canine compatibility: Leashed

dogs permitted
Fees and permits: None
Maps: USGS San Pedro, CA TOPO CD 10
Contact: Palos Verdes Peninsula Land Conservancy, P.O. Box 3247, Palos Verdes Peninsula, CA 90274; (310) 541-7613; www.pvplc.org

Finding the trailhead: To reach Portuguese Bend Preserve from the interchange of I-405 and I-110, drive south on I-110 for 7.2 miles. Take the Gaffey Street exit on the left toward San Pedro. Turn left onto Gaffey Street and drive 1.7 miles. Turn right at West 25th Street and drive 2.7 miles. Turn left onto Palos Verdes Drive South and drive 1.5 miles. Park in the dirt lot on the right-hand side of the road. GPS coordinates: N33 44.420' / W118 21.596'

The Hike

This hike combines several different routes through the southern part of Portuguese Bend Preserve. The preserve is vast, filled with great views, and loaded with wildflowers and wildlife. Portuguese Bend serves as an escape from the city that surrounds it and is a haven to threatened avian species such as the California gnatcatcher and coastal cactus wren.

This trail does not really traverse Klondike Canyon, but rather rises on a hillside above it. The hike quickly climbs

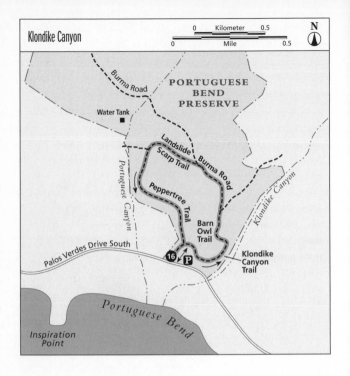

0   Kilometer   0.5

0   Mile   0.5

N

PORTUGUESE
BEND
PRESERVE

Burma Road

Water Tank ■

Portuguese Canyon

Landslide
Scarp Trail

Burma Road

Peppertree Trail

Klondike Canyon

Barn
Owl
Trail

Palos Verdes Drive South

16 P

Klondike
Canyon
Trail

Portuguese Bend

*Inspiration
Point*

400 feet in elevation above the canyon and roadway, gaining views out to Abalone Cove below, the Pacific Ocean, and Catalina Island. From there it winds around and drops back down to the roadway. This hike is a short but vigorous outing that should really get the blood pumping, and allows visitors to enjoy this beautiful preserve in a gentle, tranquil setting.

From the parking area along Palos Verdes Drive South, head through the break in the fence and turn right going up the hill. Follow the road around as it turns into a dirt path known as the Klondike Canyon Trail. At 0.4 mile turn right and connect with the Barn Owl Trail heading north.

Continue north on the Burma Road Trail/Crenshaw Boulevard and stay on the main road for 0.25 mile. Turn left at the four-way intersection onto the Landslide Scarp Trail. In 0.2 mile the trail forks again. This is the intersection with the Peppertree Trail. Take the left fork down to the main entrance road, back to the parking area.

Miles and Directions

0.0 Walk west along the dirt parking lot to the break in the fence and head up the roadway to the east.

0.15 The road becomes the Klondike Canyon Trail and heads north above the canyon.

0.4 Turn left and quickly right onto the Barn Owl Trail.

0.5 The trail becomes Burma Road Trail; follow it for 0.25 mile.

0.75 Turn left at the intersection with the Landslide Scarp Trail.

0.95 Turn left at the fork onto the Peppertree Trail. Follow the trail back to the parking area.

1.2 The Peppertree Trail intersects with a dirt road that returns to the parking area; follow it to the right.

1.5 Return to the parking area.

17 Forrestal Preserve Loop

Hike a loop around the perimeter of spectacular Forrestal
Preserve. Take in bluff views and a lovely canyon along with
coastal wildflowers.

Distance: 2-mile loop
Approximate hiking time: 1 hour
Elevation gain: 600 feet
Trail surface: Packed dirt and
dirt road
Best season: Year-round
Other trail users: Dogs, horses
Canine compatibility: Leashed
dogs permitted

Fees and permits: None
Maps: USGS San Pedro, CA
TOPO CD 10
Contact: Palos Verdes Peninsula
Land Conservancy, P.O. Box
3247, Palos Verdes Peninsula,
CA 90274; (310) 541-7613;
www.pvplc.org

Finding the trailhead: From the interchange of I-405 and I-110,
drive south on I-110 for 7.2 miles. Take the Gaffey Street exit on
the left toward San Pedro. Turn left onto Gaffey Street and drive
1.7 miles. Turn right at West 25th Street and drive 2.7 miles. Turn
left onto Palos Verdes Drive South and drive 0.6 mile. Turn right
onto Forrestal Drive; follow it for 0.7 mile to the end. Turn left onto
Intrepid Drive, and park at the end off the road. GPS coordinates:
N33 44.438' / W118 21.148'

The Hike

The southern section of the Palos Verdes Peninsula is home to
some exceedingly beautiful parcels of open land. While most
of the hiking trails are fairly well traveled, particularly by the
locals and those in the know, many areas contain some very
beautiful and somewhat incognito trails that are mostly off the
radar. This means that the hiking is exclusive and feels rather

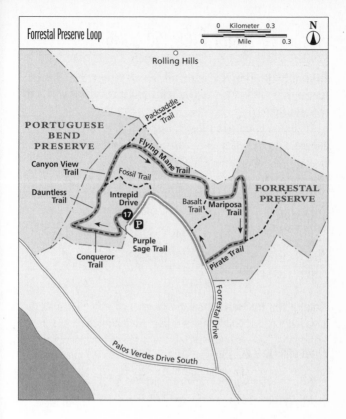

Kilometer 0.3
Mile 0.3
N

Rolling Hills

PORTUGUESE
BEND
PRESERVE

Packsaddle Trail

Flying Mane Trail

Canyon View
Trail

Fossil Trail

Dauntless
Trail

Intrepid
Drive

17

P

Basalt
Trail

Mariposa
Trail

FORRESTAL
PRESERVE

Purple
Sage Trail

Conqueror
Trail

Pirate Trail

Forrestal Drive

Palos Verdes Drive South

remote. Lovely coastal sage scrub covers the hillsides and canyons, which puts on quite a show during spring wildflower season. Monkeyflower, mariposa lily, and bush sunflower, among others, give the preserve a multicolored hue.

The preserve is also home to some endangered species, including the Palos Verdes blue butterfly, the Western tailed blue butterfly, and the California gnatcatcher, a tiny impish bird, gray in color, with a black head and beak. These three creatures, along with California rockflower, have been quite the success story for the preserve and the Palos Verdes Peninsula Land Conservancy. Critical habitat for these species has been preserved along these corridors, and the efforts have gone a long way toward conservation. It is possible that one or all of these specimens will be spotted along the trail, so wide-open eyes are a must.

From the trailhead on Intrepid Drive, hike along the Purple Sage Trail, a wide fire road that loops around and becomes the Conqueror Trail. In 0.25 mile turn right on the Dauntless Trail, which switchbacks its way up the hillside. At the Y intersection in 0.15 mile, stay left and continue up the Canyon View Trail, following it above Klondike Canyon and north of Forrestal Drive. In another 0.25 mile stay right at the second Y and continue along the Flying Mane Trail above the eroded bluffs. At the next Y intersection, in another 0.25 mile, veer left onto the Mariposa Trail and follow it for 0.35 mile. Stay right along the Pirate Trail for 0.15 mile, then follow Forrestal Drive 0.25 mile back to the parking area.

Miles and Directions

0.0 Head west along the Purple Sage Trail fire road.

0.1 Keep straight on the fire road as it becomes the Conqueror Trail.

0.25 Turn right onto the Dauntless Trail.

0.4 At the Y intersection, head left onto the Canyon View Trail.

0.65 Turn right at the Y intersection with the Flying Mane Trail.

1.0 Head left at the Y intersection with the Mariposa Trail.

1.3 Head right onto the Pirate Trail.

1.6 Turn right onto Forrestal Drive.

1.85 Turn left onto Intrepid Drive.

2.0 Return to the parking area.

18 White Point Nature Preserve/Royal Palms State Beach

Hike through an old military and missile site. The interpretive panels throughout the preserve tell the story of the natural and man-made history of the park. Then wander down to the lovely shores and tide pools of Royal Palms State Beach.

Fun hike. lots of natives... sewer!

Distance: 4-mile lollipop
Approximate hiking time: 2 hours
Elevation gain: 330 feet
Trail surface: Packed dirt
Best seasons: Spring and summer
Other trail users: Dogs, wheelchairs
Canine compatibility: Leashed

dogs permitted; no dogs on beach
Fees and permits: None
Maps: USGS Torrance, CA TOPO CD 10
Contact: Palos Verdes Peninsula Land Conservancy, P.O. Box 3247, Palos Verdes Peninsula, CA 90274; (310) 541-7613; www.pvplc.org

Finding the trailhead: To reach White Point Nature Preserve from the interchange of I-405 and I-110, drive south on I-110 for 7.2 miles. Take the Gaffey Street exit on the left toward San Pedro. Turn left onto Gaffey Street and drive 0.4 mile. Make a right onto Summerland Avenue and drive 1 mile. Turn left onto Western Avenue and drive 2.5 miles. Park along the roadway. GPS coordinates: N33 43.156' / W118 19.175'

The Hike

completed 6-22-11 w/ Mardi.

White Point Nature Preserve sits on the remains of an old Nike missile site. The Nikes were designed to work as a

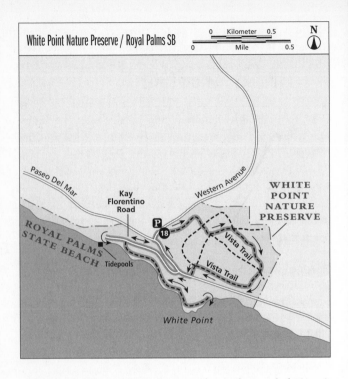

strategic defense against planes and missiles, and their primary goal was to protect large cities and urban areas. The site has been converted from a military installation into a nature preserve open to hikers, wheelchairs, and dogs. The area opened in 2003 for the public to enjoy and is loaded with interpretive panels and interesting history, along with exceedingly magnificent views of the Pacific Ocean and Catalina Island. Here visitors can enjoy the coastal sage scrub grasslands and the open air. Benches are provided so that hikers/walkers can relax and take in the atmosphere.

From the impromptu parking on Western Avenue, head through the hiking entrance and follow the trail north and east through the interior of the preserve. There is no right or wrong way to see this preserve, though the loop here includes a trip to the lovely sands and tide pools of Royal Palms State Beach. Hikers may want to fully explore and enjoy the left-over military installation, such as gun emplacements and all of the interpretive trail signs at White Point, before descending to the beach. There are quite a few interesting tidbits to read about in the preserve, and the views are magnificent.

From the preserve, cross Paseo del Mar and drop down along Kay Florentino Road to the beach. The tide pools are to the west and the sands are to the east. Retrace your steps to the car, and enjoy some of the best hiking and sights the South Bay has to offer.

Miles and Directions

0.0 Head east and north from the parking on Western Avenue.

0.2 Turn right and cross the paved Vista Trail.

0.3 Turn left at the four-way intersection.

0.4 Turn right at the next four-way intersection onto the Vista Interpretive Trail.

0.6 Turn right and stay on the Vista Interpretive Trail.

1.1 Turn left and exit onto Paseo del Mar, then turn right and walk west.

1.25 Turn left onto Kay Florentino Road. Walk to the tide pools.

1.7 Turn east and walk along the beach.

2.25 Arrive at White Point.

2.4 Turn around.

3.2 Turn right onto Kay Florentino Road.

3.6 Turn left onto Paseo del Mar.

3.85 Turn right onto Western Avenue.

4.0 Arrive back at parking.

About the Author

Allen Riedel is a photographer, journalist, author, and teacher. He writes an outdoor column for the *Press Enterprise* and has authored several hiking guides, including *Best Easy Day Hikes Riverside* and *Best Easy Day Hikes San Bernardino* for FalconGuides, as well as *Best Hikes with Dogs in Southern California* and *100 Classic Hikes in Southern California,*. He lives with his wife, Monique, and children, Michael, Sierra, and Makaila, in Riverside, California.